THE MIRACLES
OF CHRIST

WHAT LIVING BEYOND
THE IMPOSSIBLE LOOKS LIKE

The Miracles of Christ: What Living Beyond the Impossible Looks Like

Contents of this book include excerpts from *Living Amazed: How Divine Encounters Can Change Your Life*, copyright © 2017 by James Robison; Published by Revell

Copyright© 2018 by Inprov, Ltd.
ISBN: 978-0-9995389-2-0

For further information, write Inprov, at:
2150 E. Continental Blvd, Southlake, TX 76092

CONTENTS

From the beginning of my life, I have been a witness to countless miracles. In fact, I consider my own life to be a miracle itself. Betty and I have both seen miraculous things, and I believe God wants all believers to see and experience miracles today. In fact, God may even use you for a miracle!

Miracles happened in the Bible, but they continue happening today. Whether a miraculous healing, a divine intervention, or a supernatural shift, God is ever-present and constantly at work.

When we yield to Him and His heavenly will over our lives, we can live a miraculous life. God desires to bless you and reveal His miracle power to you! I pray that you are encouraged and inspired by the stories and testimonies of the miracles of Christ!

James Robison

WHAT IS A MIRACLE?

A miracle is generally thought of as something that occurs outside of earth's natural laws. A miracle can't be explained by science or nature. It's a supernatural event of divine origin. We see miracles throughout scripture, both in the Old and New Testaments, and miracles are still happening today.

Everywhere Jesus went during His time on earth, people were amazed by what He did and what He said. They were amazed by His wisdom and teaching. They were amazed by His authority over nature, illness, and demons. And they were amazed by His miraculous healing power. Sometimes, people were amazed simply by His presence.

From "let there be light" to the miracle of Christ's resurrection, from the miracles the apostles witnessed and experienced as they travelled with the Messiah to the miracles I've observed throughout my own life, I believe that God has miracles of all kinds in store for everyone. We may not all see or encounter the same things, but

anyone can experience a miracle.

And He can use you to be someone else's miracle. Sometimes that's the best way to see our own miracle come to fruition—to be the answer to someone else's.

Throughout the Bible and down through the ages, He has used flawed, weak, and wayward people to pour out His power and accomplish His purpose on earth. I truly believe that God continues working miracles even today, always pointing us back to Him and reminding us of who He is: a faithful Father—sovereign, just, and full of love for His children. When we witness miracles, we witness a revelation of His character and His love for us.

As you read this book, I hope you will see that miracles are a manifestation of God's love and power pouring out over His creation. And I hope you will also see that sometimes we don't get the miracle that we're praying for, but that doesn't mean that there isn't a different one He has in store.

I believe that God
has a purpose
and plan for everyone.
The body of Christ contains
no small, unimportant,
or insignificant members.

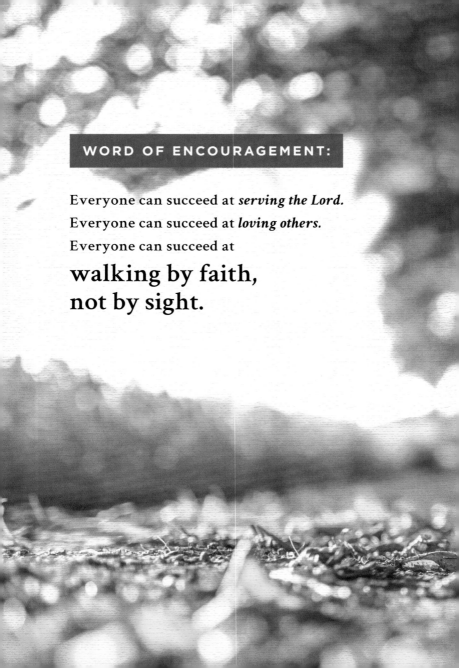

WORD OF ENCOURAGEMENT:

Everyone can succeed at *serving the Lord.*
Everyone can succeed at *loving others.*
Everyone can succeed at

walking by faith, not by sight.

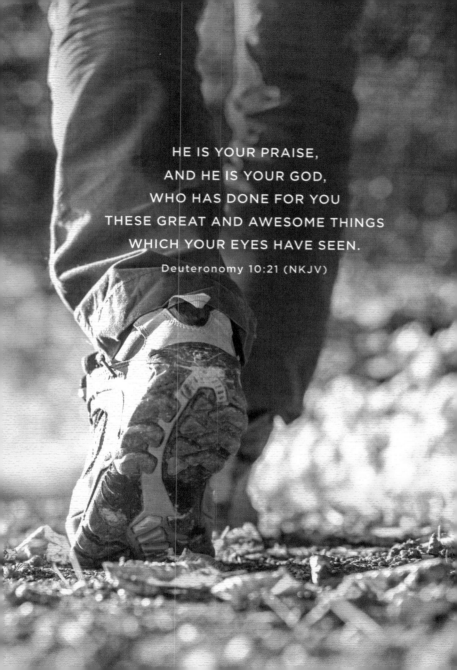

HE IS YOUR PRAISE,
AND HE IS YOUR GOD,
WHO HAS DONE FOR YOU
THESE GREAT AND AWESOME THINGS
WHICH YOUR EYES HAVE SEEN.
Deuteronomy 10:21 (NKJV)

"You talk about Jesus Christ?" the woman in the brothel asked. I told her that I did. "Make my sister walk," she said, pointing to a woman sitting on the floor. "That is my sister. She hasn't walked in four years. And for the last 15 days she hasn't moved off of that floor. She is dying."

I told the Lord, "I've seen blind people see, deaf people hear, crooked backs straighten, skin disease fall off of bodies. Make this woman walk. Do this for You, not for me."

I said, "Okay, we will pray," and asked some other ladies to massage the legs of the woman on the mat. We prayed for about five minutes and I said,

"Get up and walk in Jesus' name."

She hobbled across the room then sat in a plastic chair with armrests, still in a lot of pain. She could move her legs a little bit, but they were stiff. I looked at her sister and knew this wasn't a miracle. This wasn't going to convince anybody of anything.

"I want to pray more," I said. About three minutes later, the crippled woman's countenance changed. She had a glow and a strength come across her. She grabbed the chair's armrests and said, "Alright, I'm ready! I'm ready!"

I told her, "No, no. We have to pray more!" She insisted that she was ready, but I kept telling her, "Not yet! Not yet!" After two more minutes, I told her that she could get up.

The woman got up and began to walk. Then she began to jump up and down. Her sister couldn't believe it and went to the wall of gods, put her hands together, and began to thank them.

As the woman prayed to her Hindu gods, I asked her, "Haven't you been praying to your gods for four years that your sister would walk?" She said that she had and I told her, "That was Jesus Christ. Jesus healed your sister." It turned out that the woman who was healed that day was not just any old woman; she was the woman who started that entire block of brothels in Mumbai and Jesus changed her life!

Copyright © Nick Vujicic, 2010.

PERFECT...

God uses imperfect people to accomplish His perfect will! We can trust that God is in control, and He knows every outcome. He has a perfect will for each of our lives.

PRAYER:

Today we ask to be reminded that we can be someone else's miracle. Sometimes we get wrapped up in looking for the answers to our own prayers and forget that we can be an instrument in answering someone else's. Thank you, Father, for allowing us that opportunity, and let us not lose sight of it today! Amen.

God wants us to become good noticers of His creation and the miracles that are just right in front of us. When we open our eyes to the beauty in His creation, we **see the miracles of Christ** all around us. There is nothing to compare to that experience.

THEN MOSES STRETCHED OUT HIS HAND OVER THE SEA; AND THE LORD CAUSED THE SEA TO GO BACK BY A STRONG EAST WIND ALL THAT NIGHT, AND MADE THE SEA INTO DRY LAND, AND THE WATERS WERE DIVIDED.

Exodus 14:21 (NKJV)

A lot of times we say, "I'm tired," but really it is not that we're tired, because if you're tired you can take a nap and feel better. It's that we're depleted. We're depleted physically, mentally, emotionally, and spiritually.

A depleted condition is a vulnerable condition. A run-down body is susceptible to sickness. A weary mind lacks focus and resolve. Battered emotions leave us wounded and empty. And a tired spirit falls easily to temptation.

A true Sabbath occurs when we stop laboring and allow God to replenish us in every way. Too often, we think we can go seven days a week. But God himself set the pattern for us. We are certainly not more powerful than He!

When Jesus Christ walked the earth, He often removed Himself from the crowds. We're familiar with the time He miraculously fed five thousand families, but we don't usually remember the context. Just before that day, Jesus' beloved cousin John (called "John the Baptist") was beheaded by King Herod. Jesus withdrew to a secluded place, but people discovered where He was and a huge crowd sought Him out. That's why there were so many people in a remote place with no food.

Jesus felt compassion toward them and healed the sick all day long. As the hour became late, they grew hungry, prompting the dinner miracle. After they had all eaten, Jesus sent the crowds home and even sent His disciples on their way. Matthew's gospel tells us, "Immediately He made the disciples get into the boat and go ahead of Him to the other side, while He sent the crowds away. After He had sent the crowds away, He went up on the mountain by Himself to pray; and when it was evening, He was there alone" (Matthew 14:23).

We must not neglect a time of rest.

We need the renewal of our mind, body, and spirit.

HEAL . . .

Sometimes miracles come in the form of healing. Scripture tells us that by His stripes, we are healed (see Isaiah 53:5). We know that wholeness awaits us in heaven, regardless of the sickness or ailments we experience on earth. We also know that God performs miraculous healings.

Whether physical, emotional, relational, or spiritual, everyone could use some healing from time to time. Trust in His ability and willingness to bring health and wholeness to every area of your life; know that He has the power to heal!

PRAYER:

God, help us to remember the importance of making time for rest in our lives. You gave us the Sabbath for a reason. And you teach us that rest brings renewal, fresh vision, insight, and understanding. It is through this renewal that we can gain a better appreciation for the plans you have for our lives and can see the beauty of the miracles you work all around us! Amen.

When I was old enough to understand, my mother told me the circumstances of my birth and that the Lord had told her,

"Have this baby; it will bring joy to the world."

There is nothing to compare to that experience. God was working miracles for my life before I was even born. I feel so blessed to be on the receiving end of such a miraculous circumstance, and I feel led to be a blessing to others. I pray that God allows me to be part of someone else's miracle!

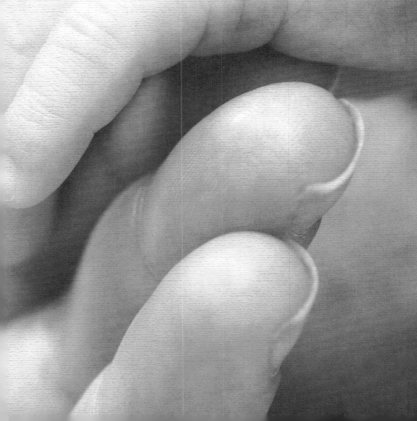

BUT JESUS LOOKED AT THEM AND SAID TO THEM, "WITH MEN THIS IS IMPOSSIBLE, BUT WITH GOD ALL THINGS ARE POSSIBLE."

Matthew 19:26 (NKJV)

Christians don't pray for one another like we should. We don't have an active faith that believes He is the same yesterday, today, and forever; that He can still do miracles and heal. We ought to be doing what the Bible says—laying hands on the sick and praying for them—and it shouldn't be left up to Oral Roberts, or anyone else, to have lines of people coming for healing prayer. We should be ministering to the needs of people in our local congregations.

A MIRACLE'S TIMING

It's a miracle I was ever born. In fact, if the laws
we have today were in effect back then, I'm 99.99
percent certain I would have been aborted.

My mother worked as a practical nurse, giving
hospice care to homebound individuals. She had been
married at a young age, but by the time she was forty,

she was long divorced and working in the home of an elderly man in Houston. That man had an alcoholic son, about ten years younger than my mother, who one day forced himself on her and raped her.

It is truly a miracle that I was born, and my life continues to be miraculous. From the circumstances of my birth and childhood, growing up in poverty without a father, most people never would have believed that my life would be as it is today.

It's a miracle that I made it through so many of the experiences I did. And I believe my journey from childhood to adulthood is such a testimony to the way

God can use anyone!

My story isn't standalone, either. I've spoken with so many people who have been through difficult circumstances—broken families, lost loved ones, isolation in some of the darkest pits—but God doesn't turn His back on us. He reaches into the pit, shines His light, and pulls us out in miraculous ways.

Every miracle I've experienced has completely occurred within God's timing.

When we trust in His will and yield our lives to Him, we see that His timing is always perfect.

We may be impatient or begin to think that we know what's best, but a miracle's timing is something that only the Father knows. The timing of a miracle isn't something that we can predict, know, or control, but it is something that can result in an amazing show of God's power and sovereignty.

When we trust in God's timing
for the miracles we're praying for,
we will begin to see what living
beyond the impossible
really looks like.

In Acts 3, Peter and John were instrumental in releasing a miraculous demonstration of God's power to heal. Even the unbelieving public called it a notable miracle. When they were questioned and challenged by some observers, these bold witnesses proclaimed, "It is the power in the name of Jesus." The key verse, the absolutely essential power necessary to become bold witnesses is found in Acts 4:31: "And when they had prayed, the place where they had gathered together was shaken, and they were all filled with the Holy Spirit and began to speak the word of God with boldness." If we are going to see a positive impact made on our personal, local, and national lives because of the effect of bold witnesses, it will be because,

we have experienced the same power.

Excerpted from The Stream: Refreshing Hearts and Minds, Renewing Freedom's Blessing © 2016 by James Robison. Published by Worthy Publishing. All rights reserved.

NOW TO HIM WHO IS ABLE
TO DO IMMEASURABLY MORE
THAN ALL WE ASK OR IMAGINE,
ACCORDING TO HIS POWER
THAT IS AT WORK WITHIN US,
TO HIM BE GLORY IN THE CHURCH
AND IN CHRIST JESUS
THROUGHOUT ALL GENERATIONS,
FOR EVER AND EVER! AMEN.

Ephesians 3:20-21 (NIV)

Do you know why most of us don't experience miracles? It's because we never put ourselves in situations that necessitate one! We comfort the grieving instead of calling people out of the tomb. But if we took a few more risks, we might see a few more miracles! And that's one more secret to experiencing the miraculous: you have to risk your reputation.

Isn't that what Shadrach, Meshach, and Abednego did when they refused to bow down to a ninety-foot idol?

They knew they'd be executed if they didn't bow down, but they feared God more than they feared death itself. They would rather die by the flame than dishonor God.

To be honest, I could've come up with a dozen rationalizations to justify bowing down. But it's our rationalizations that often annul His miraculous intervention.

When we compromise our integrity, we don't leave room for divine intervention. When we take matters into our own hands, we take God out of the equation. When we try to manipulate a situation, we miss out on the miracle.

Stop and think about it.

If Shadrach, Meshach, and Abednego had bowed down to the statue, they would have been delivered from the fiery furnace. But it would have been by the hand of man, not the hand of God. And while they would have saved their lives, they would have sacrificed their integrity. They also would have forfeited the miracle.

When we bow to what's wrong, we put our reputation and God's reputation at risk. But when we stand up for what's right, we establish God's reputation by putting ourselves in a posture where God can show up and show off. And God does just that.

Excerpted from The Grave Robber © *2014 by Mark Batterson.*
Published by Baker Books, a division of Baker Publishing Group.
Used by permission.

CONFIDENCE...

We can have confidence in God's power and timing. He is a God of promise and can be trusted.

Hebrews 4:16 encourages us to "approach God's throne of grace with confidence." Have confidence in His power and trust in His timing!

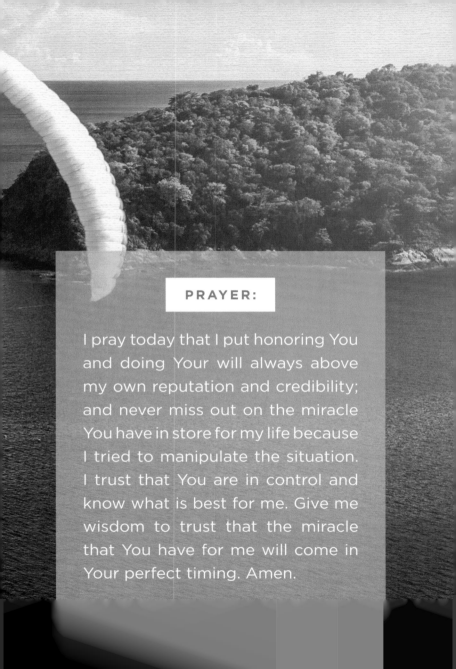

PRAYER:

I pray today that I put honoring You and doing Your will always above my own reputation and credibility; and never miss out on the miracle You have in store for my life because I tried to manipulate the situation. I trust that You are in control and know what is best for me. Give me wisdom to trust that the miracle that You have for me will come in Your perfect timing. Amen.

Things happen, maybe not as fast as we want; our timing is so different from God's. I've learned that miracles I've seen in my life personally, sometimes it seemed like it was a long time before I got what I had asked for.

But it was because God

wanted to show me some other things along the way that I would have missed maybe if I had gone straight to what I wanted.

—*Betty Robison*

Amazement is a good word to describe the common experience of the early Christians. Something new happened in history regarding the fulfillment of Old Testament promises and it was truly amazing. It had started out rather inconspicuously with John the Baptist preaching to the remnant of Israel far away from the large cities. He then introduced Jesus who had been born in a manger, raised in a small country town, and began His ministry hanging with common men like fishermen. But the tension built as the religious leaders became jealous and tried to eliminate Him. Finally, He confronted Pilate, Herod, and Caiaphas before His crucifixion, then was resurrected on the first day of the week. After that, the disciples were constantly amazed at what they saw and experienced.

A new creation was introduced in His resurrection. The Jews believed that one day God would invade history with His kingdom, but they thought it was probably a long time off. They were still convinced that Jesus was not what they had been promised. But the disciples of Jesus were daily amazed. Lives were being transformed. Some were healed. Demons were cast out. Governments were afraid. The apostles' preaching was accompanied by miracles of all types. Truly heaven and earth had come together.

What happened to that amazement? Some biblical scholars have concluded that God withdrew His miraculous power after the original apostles died and the canon of scripture was completed. But that is conjecture and is contradicted by the continuation of amazing phenomena in some places throughout history. A better explanation is that we have been willing to settle for amusement instead of amazement.

The good news that the King has come and a new day has dawned is being proclaimed and heard. People who have been sedated with amusement are awaking to the amazement of living as God's new creation people now. Like the early believers, they expect the miraculous when heaven and earth meet.

He is still amazing. Let's look away from our amusement to the One our hearts long to know.

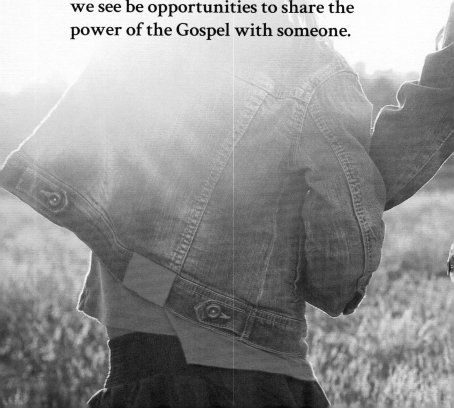

WITNESS . . .

When we experience a miracle or play a part in one, we are called to witness. May we never take a miracle for granted or become complacent after witnessing His miraculous power. Rather, let us be witnesses for His glory! Let the miracles we see be opportunities to share the power of the Gospel with someone.

PRAYER:

God, open our eyes to the miraculous works all around us. Let our hearts not settle for amusement, but let us seek the amazement that You provide. We want to live in awe of You. Let us pray as the early believers did.

Lord, look upon their threats and grant to Your servants that with all boldness they may speak Your word, by stretching out Your hand to heal, and that signs and wonders may be done through the name of Your holy Servant Jesus. (Acts 4:29-30, NKJV) Let us be amazed and bold! Amen.

Persevere in your prayers. We don't have the foresight to see what will pan out in God's timing, but we know that we can continue coming to Him with our heart's desires.

When you grow weary, turn to Him for renewal. When you feel weak, let Him be your strength. When you are lost, remember that **He is your light in the dark.**

WHAT JESUS DID HERE IN CANA OF GALILEE
WAS THE FIRST OF THE SIGNS THROUGH
WHICH HE REVEALED HIS GLORY;
AND HIS DISCIPLES BELIEVED IN HIM.

John 2:11 (NIV)

It is an honor and privilege
when God allows me to play
a part in blessing someone else.
I always say that I am
blessed to be a blessing.
When I yield my life to Him,
He often uses me to bless others,
and I end up being blessed, too.

THE MIRACLES OF CHRIST

Christ's time on earth was filled with miracles that are documented throughout Scripture. With these miracles, He healed people, transformed lives and began the work of building God's Kingdom on earth. The illustrations of Christ's miracles in Scripture show us that even from the beginning, God has wanted to be present in our lives on earth—He orchestrates divine appointments and supernaturally intervenes. What an amazing Father we have.

We can look back at the miracles of Christ and see expressions of God's love, power, and sovereignty. And while Christ is no longer physically walking on earth, miracles are still happening today through the power of the Holy Spirit. God reveals that He is still with us, that He is still working miracles all around us, and that we can always turn to Him in prayer and fellowship and trust in His provision for our lives.

As we look at the miracles of Christ, both in Scripture and modern-day, we find confirmation that God is who He says He is. He is omnipresent, sovereign, and full of love. He has the power to heal the sick, make the blind see, raise the dead. He transforms hearts and saves lives!

Miracles, even praying for a miracle, point us back to Christ and put us in a position of standing firmly on God's promises.

Miracles draw us closer to Christ.

As He works miracles in our lives in His time and in His way, we are reminded that His plan is to prosper us. These truths are revealed in the miracles of Christ—every healing, every salvation—we see His love poured out, people covered in His grace and mercy.

As you take a closer look at the miracles of Christ, what truths are revealed about the Father's heart? What is it about miracles that push you closer to Jesus? How can you become a better witness of His glory?

Miracles
point us back
to Christ.

One of the greatest miracles a person can ever experience is the supernatural act of redemption. God can take the biggest mess of a person and completely transform their heart and life. He can pull someone from the pit of hell and put them on the **road to complete restoration.**

SO THE KING GAVE THE ORDER, AND THEY BROUGHT DANIEL AND THREW HIM INTO THE LIONS' DEN. THE KIND SAID TO DANIEL, "MAY YOUR GOD, WHOM YOU SERVE CONTINUALLY, RESCUE YOU!" WHEN [THE KING] CAME NEAR THE DEN [THE NEXT MORNING] HE CALLED TO DANIEL IN AN ANGUISHED VOICE, "DANIEL, SERVANT OF THE LIVING GOD, HAS YOUR GOD, WHOM YOU SERVE CONTINUALLY, BEEN ABLE TO RESCUE YOU FROM THE LIONS?" DANIEL ANSWERED, "MAY THE KING LIVE FOREVER! MY GOD SENT HIS ANGEL, AND HE SHUT THE MOUTHS OF THE LIONS. THEY HAVE NOT HURT ME, BECAUSE I WAS FOUND INNOCENT IN HIS SIGHT. NOR HAVE I EVER DONE ANY WRONG BEFORE YOU, YOUR MAJESTY."

Daniel 6:16, 20-22 (NIV)

Simon Peter has been criticized over the years for his brash personality, his denial of Christ on the morning of the crucifixion, and his impetuous actions. And he is often criticized for the lack of faith he showed in this account.

But I'd like to look at Peter's actions more closely. The passage says, "Peter called to him, 'Lord, if it's really you, tell me to come to you, walking on the water.' 'Yes, come,' Jesus said. So Peter went over the side of the boat."

Yes, I know there's more to come, and I know the next verse talks about Peter's faith faltering, but for now let's focus on what happened first. And let me ask you a question: Would you have gotten out of the boat?

Remember the seas were churning, the winds were howling and contrary, and the boat was rocking from side to side. The disciples were terrified. And then a ghostlike figure appeared on the horizon, a figure that turned out to be Jesus walking on water. Would your first move be to go "over the side of the boat?" That was Peter's first impulse.

We refer to this passage as the miracle of Jesus walking on water. We would do well to recognize this also as the miracle of Peter walking on water. He looked into the eyes of Jesus, and he was the only disciple—by faith—to get out of the boat!

Sometimes you have to be willing to be the one to get out of the boat.

There are times when you have to step out in faith, and no one else follows, and you feel all alone. That's when God grows your faith more than ever.

The storm you're facing right now may not be something you just need to survive. Very possibly the troubles in front of you are a remarkable opportunity for you to experience a great miracle.

You'll never find your miracle if you stay hunkered down in the boat.

Excerpted from Find Your Miracle © *2016 by Kerry Shook and Chris Shook. Excerpted by permission of WaterBrook, a division of Penguin Random House, LLC. All rights reserved.*

SUPPLIER . . .

God is the supplier of all our needs.
Philippians 4:19 assures us that our needs
will be met by God. We can trust in
this promise. That doesn't mean we are
entitled to a miracle, but it does mean that
we can have faith that our true needs will
be met. He is a faithful supplier.

PRAYER:

God, let us learn from Peter. Today we pray that we have a miracle moment of walking on water, of trusting You and getting out of our boat in the midst of the storm; having faith big enough to walk with You through the worst of it. Thank you, God, for being the calm in every storm and for always seeing us through to the other side. Thank you that, with You, we too can experience the miracle of walking on water. Amen.

At one time in my life, I had many miraculous experiences and became so enriched by my faith in

God's healing power.

I knew that healing was real and began to study the Word of God on the subject. And I became zealous for what God said. In fact, I became so caught up in the truth of God's Word that I could no longer hear the doubts and skepticism of other people—their vain speculations, assertions, and fruitless discussions.

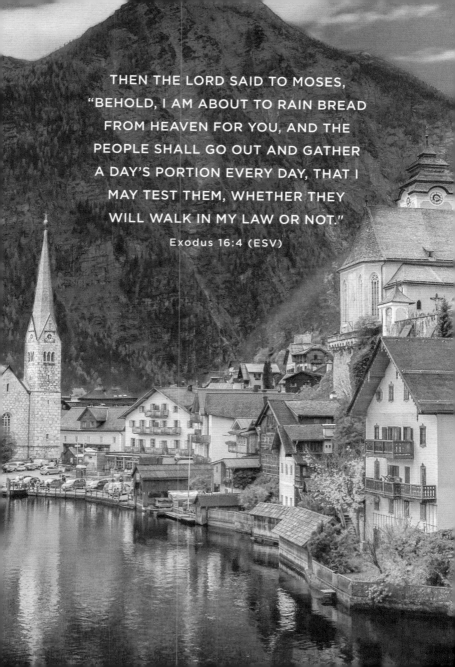

THEN THE LORD SAID TO MOSES,
"BEHOLD, I AM ABOUT TO RAIN BREAD
FROM HEAVEN FOR YOU, AND THE
PEOPLE SHALL GO OUT AND GATHER
A DAY'S PORTION EVERY DAY, THAT I
MAY TEST THEM, WHETHER THEY
WILL WALK IN MY LAW OR NOT."

Exodus 16:4 (ESV)

Why are we able to ask an all-powerful, all-knowing, all-seeing God for help? Why can we ask for a better life and future with Him? There's really only one reason. The reason is the object of our faith. Because of this object, we can boldly come to God with our needs and wants and receive answers. It is not faith in and of itself. We don't put stock in the fact that we know how to believe. It's the object of our faith: Jesus. It's in Him that we put our faith. It's not in our amazing confession or how good we are at asking or believing. It's all about Him. It's because of who He is that we can continue asking, even when we've heard "no" or "wait" in the past.

Walking into God's plan and truly living by faith come by understanding that Jesus is the source of our faith. "By grace you have been saved, through faith—and this is not from yourselves, it is the gift of God" (Ephesians 2:8).

This grace that has saved us is not some principle.

Grace is a person. It's Jesus.

And it's not ourselves and our amazing faith that

transforms our lives: it's this grace from Jesus. All our confidence and all our faith have to be wrapped up in the Son. Because of Him, we can approach God, ask with boldness, and see mountains move. Because of Him, we don't have to beat ourselves up for that relationship we let go on too long or that job opportunity that fizzled. Because of Him, we can dream differently and see those God-ordained dreams come to fruition.

The father in Matthew 17 knew the disciples weren't the source. When things didn't work out at the church, he went straight to Jesus to ask for help. It's time for all of us to go straight to the source with complete confidence that He can move any mountain and help us walk into our future. Let's go straight to Jesus and make the Big Ask.

What are you asking God for? Don't wait to get to heaven one day and wish that you would've believed for more. Don't arrive at eternity and wish you would've asked for more in this life. Doubt and the Devil say, "Wait for tomorrow." Faith and the Father say, "Ask today."

Taken from Faith Forward Future © 2017 by Chad Veach.
Used by permission of Thomas Nelson.

FREE . . .

Because of Jesus, we can experience true freedom. In fact, the Bible tells us that "where the Spirit of the Lord is, there is freedom" (2 Corinthians 3:17, ESV). There may be something that you feel is a hindrance in your life—a sickness, a difficult circumstance, a broken relationship—but because of Jesus we are free! Live and walk in that freedom and believe that nothing of this world can hold you back from the glory He has in store for your life.

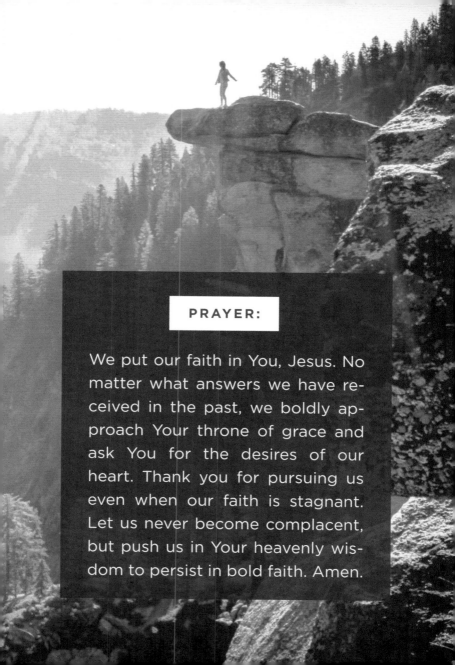

PRAYER:

We put our faith in You, Jesus. No matter what answers we have received in the past, we boldly approach Your throne of grace and ask You for the desires of our heart. Thank you for pursuing us even when our faith is stagnant. Let us never become complacent, but push us in Your heavenly wisdom to persist in bold faith. Amen.

"What do you want me to do for you?" Jesus asked him.
The blind man said, *"Rabbi, I want to see."*
Just as Jesus asks Bartimaeus, He is asking
us, *"What do you want me to do for you?"* Jesus
wants to hear you ask for the desires of
your heart. When we ask to see,

He wants to show us the truth and light.

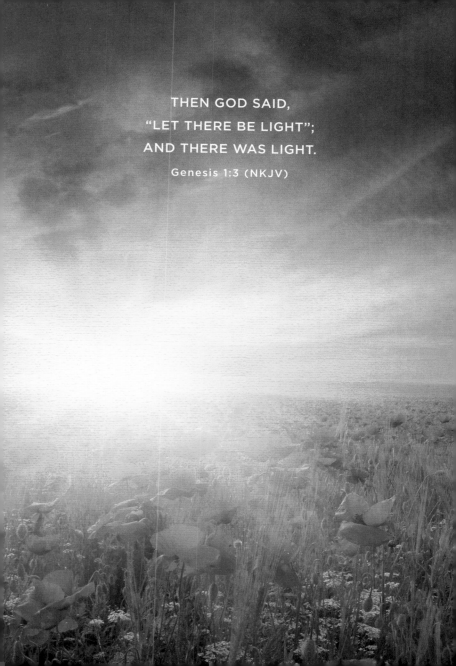

THEN GOD SAID,
"LET THERE BE LIGHT";
AND THERE WAS LIGHT.

Genesis 1:3 (NKJV)

Let us not get distracted
by doubt or skepticism,
but let us stand firm
on Your promises.
Allow us to maintain
a zeal for Your Word
and shine a light
for others who are lost
in the darkness of
defeat and doubt.

WHEN A MIRACLE DOESN'T HAPPEN

Sometimes we pray and believe for a miracle and it doesn't happen. We understand that miracles happen in God's timing and in His way, but what does it mean when we don't get the miracle? How do we react when our prayers go unanswered?

In my life, I have seen the most miraculous

things—things that some people might not even believe! God is so wonderful, and His heart for us is so huge. I've also experienced some of the deepest heartache a person can experience.

We all know that sometimes physical healing doesn't happen, and we have to ask God instead for the miracle of healing our broken hearts. I can't ever talk about answered prayer without thinking about the prayers we prayed for our beautiful daughter, Robin, who died of cancer at the age of forty. She never once wavered in her faith, and neither did we. And yet she died.

Sometimes we have to pray for the grace of God to help us walk through the pain

of not getting our desired miracle and not understanding why. Betty and I learned that lesson firsthand. Prayer may not operate on our time frame or our schedule, and it may not be up to our expectations, but it's still a miracle in action. So we must pray.

When we navigate the waters of not getting the

miracle we prayed for, we see that Jesus is much more than just a source for miracles. We are reminded that Jesus is our source of comfort, calm, peace, joy, and purpose. And our love for God is not reliant upon an answered prayer or a supernatural miracle. Above all, God is sovereign, and even when we don't understand why we don't get the miracle we're praying for, we can trust that His plan is bigger and we are loved.

We know that
we will never have
all the answers,
but we find peace
in knowing that Jesus
is the ultimate Healer.

Without question, God could have healed
Robin—right up until the moment when
she stepped through into eternity. He can do
anything. But can God also, through the loss
of our precious daughter, help us to bind up
more broken hearts because our own hearts
have been shattered? I pray He does, because
that's what Betty and I want to do, and our
hearts have certainly been broken. And all the
people who cared for us and wept with us—

**they helped to bind up
our hearts.**

BUT THESE ARE WRITTEN SO THAT YOU
MAY CONTINUE TO BELIEVE THAT JESUS IS
THE MESSIAH, THE SON OF GOD, AND THAT
BY BELIEVING IN HIM YOU WILL HAVE LIFE
BY THE POWER OF HIS NAME.

John 20:31 (NLT)

When you go through a time where God doesn't come through like you think He should, I think it's okay to express your anger to God. I talked to a young man whose wife was diagnosed with cancer and they'd just been married; Stage 3 cancer. He came to us. We prayed with him and he said, "I'm really mad at God. And everybody tells me, 'Don't get mad at God."

I said, "That's okay as long as you pour it out to Him. Because He loves you and He's big enough to handle it. Pour out your anger and your hurt and your grief." The only thing you shouldn't do is turn away from Him because that is kind of what we want to do when He doesn't come through; we're disappointed.

I know in scripture Mary was disappointed when Jesus didn't come right away to heal her brother Lazarus. She didn't understand. She believed in Him so much and she knew He was going to come through and He loved them, and then He didn't. It says that she stayed at home when Martha ran out to meet Him. Then Jesus asked for her. Martha came back and said, "The teacher is asking for you."

I love that when we turn away from Him He's still coming to us; He's still asking for us. There are so many questions we'll never be able to answer until we get to heaven, but the good news is He is the answer.

His presence is with us.

The ultimate miracle is Jesus. It's not the presents that He gives us, it's His presence. That's the only way we can make it when it doesn't happen the way we think it should.

Excerpted from LIFE TODAY *taping*
with Kerry & Chris Shook, January 23, 2017.

PRESENCE . . .

The ultimate miracle is Jesus. It's not the presents that He gives; it's His presence. Even when things don't turn out the way we think they should, we are still blessed with the presence of our Father and the peace He brings.

PRAYER:

God, sometimes we don't get the miracle we're praying for. We believe You can work the miracle, and trust You have the power to move mountains, but it just doesn't happen. Today we pray that even when we don't understand, we continue to trust You, continue to find comfort in Your presence, and continue to come to You with our prayers. We acknowledge that we don't have all the answers or understand why things may or may not happen, but we know that You are God, and that is more than enough. Amen.

Don't be discouraged if you don't see the miracle you are praying for.

God always has the final word, but we should be praying boldly for the sick and the suffering. We should be asking God to perform miracles. We should be trusting Him for His mercy, wisdom, and grace. And if we don't see the miracles we're praying for, we can still trust God for the miracle that enables us to walk in peace, hope, and faith, even with the pain that accompanies loss.

JESUS LOOKED HER IN THE EYE.
"DIDN'T I TELL YOU THAT IF YOU BELIEVED,
YOU WOULD SEE THE GLORY OF GOD?"
THEN, TO THE OTHERS, "GO AHEAD, TAKE AWAY
THE STONE." THEY REMOVED THE STONE.
JESUS RAISED HIS EYES TO HEAVEN AND PRAYED,
"FATHER, I'M GRATEFUL THAT YOU HAVE LISTENED TO
ME. I KNOW YOU ALWAYS DO LISTEN, BUT ON ACCOUNT
OF THIS CROWD STANDING HERE I'VE SPOKEN SO THAT
THEY MIGHT BELIEVE THAT YOU SENT ME." THEN HE
SHOUTED, "LAZARUS, COME OUT!" AND HE CAME OUT,
A CADAVER, WRAPPED FROM HEAD TO TOE, AND
WITH A KERCHIEF OVER HIS FACE. JESUS TOLD THEM,
"UNWRAP HIM AND LET HIM LOOSE."

John 11:40-44 (MSG)

God is still the God of what's left. You may not feel this to be true, but if you hold onto your faith, God is going to use the rubble, the tears and the heartache for a greater purpose.

Amos 3:12 (NKJV) paints a great picture, though when you first read it, it might seem strange: "As a shepherd takes from the mouth of a lion two legs or a piece of an ear, so shall the children of Israel be taken out who dwell in Samaria—in the corner of the bed and on the edge of the couch!"

A beautiful allegory is being painted in the first part of this passage. A lion had devoured a lamb. And the only thing left for the shepherd to salvage was two legs and a piece of an ear. It did not matter how broken the lamb was or that what was left seemed hardly worth the trouble; the shepherd fought for what was left. To him, the remains were significant. They mattered. They had purpose.

They were worth redeeming.

If you are hurt, weighed down by trouble or struggling through family conflict, it is not over. You may not have what you used to have. Your life may look different. But you are not finished.

If you still have an ear to hear and a leg to stand on, you can stand on God's Word. You can find hope in the promise that "though your beginning was small, yet your latter end would increase abundantly" (Job 8:7 NKJV).

When hell tries to decimate your relationships with your loved ones, it is easy to let bulldozers come and topple the broken walls that are barely left standing. But stand up and fight for what is left.

Talk again. Pray again. Try again. Forgive again. Reach out again. Go to dinner again. Refuse to give up. Refuse to allow depression and worry and anxiety and frustration to overcome. Fill your valley with prayer. Fill it with praise. Fill it with Scripture.

The miracle is not found in what was lost. The miracle is found in what you've got left.

Excerpted from Love Like You've Never Been Hurt © *2018 by Jentezen Franklin. Published by Chosen Books, a division of Baker Publishing Group. Used by permission.*

PURPOSE . . .

We trust in the Father's purpose. He has a purpose for every life, for every miracle, for every time that we don't get the miracle we're praying for. We trust that His purpose is bigger and better than anything we can ever plan for, even when we don't understand.

Father, on the days when we feel most like Mary, disappointed that Jesus wasn't there sooner or didn't come through with the miracle we prayed for, help us to look at what's left. Help us see the miracle we didn't know we needed. And, show us how to use this experience to bless those around us. Father, help us to touch the lives of others, and in turn, we know that we, too, have received Your touch. Amen.

Losing our daughter hasn't changed my view of God's miraculous healing—or my belief in God's desire to see people healed and made whole . . .

Our healing lies in the object of our faith—Almighty God—

not in the size or strength of our faith.

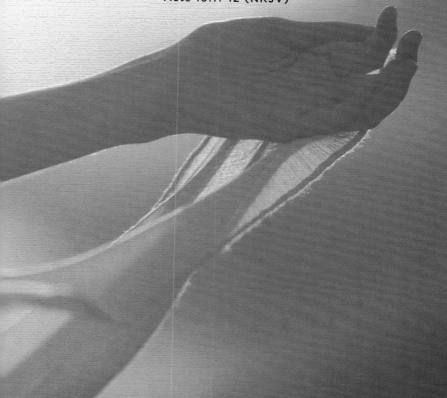

NOW GOD WORKED UNUSUAL MIRACLES
BY THE HANDS OF PAUL, SO THAT EVEN
HANDKERCHIEFS OR APRONS WERE BROUGHT
FROM HIS BODY TO THE SICK, AND THE
DISEASES LEFT THEM AND THE EVIL SPIRITS
WENT OUT OF THEM.

Acts 19:11-12 (NKJV)

The Lord makes all things new.
He is a God of renewal and
resurrection—He breathes life
into decay and pours light
into the darkness.

THE POSITION OF A MIRACLE

Just like there is no amount of good work we can do to earn a spot in heaven or garner our salvation, there is nothing we can do to earn a miracle.

Some people think, *"If only I pray this much,"* or *"If I just do X, Y, and Z,"* that they will get their miracle.

But God doesn't work like that. Some people

experience a miracle without ever asking for one, and some people faithfully pray for a miracle and never see it come to pass. This is a reflection of God's sovereignty—

we don't have to understand why a miracle happens or doesn't happen, but we can trust that God is in control.

Even though there is nothing we can do to earn a miracle, we can always be in a position and posture to receive a miracle or be part of one.

And even if we don't get the miracle that we're praying for, our posture can open the gates for another miracle. Maybe it's one that we aren't aware that we need, or maybe it's one that will allow us to be a miracle for someone else. When we open ourselves to the possibilities, the Holy Spirit can move and work in us and let us be a witness for something even greater than we could ever imagine.

The biggest part of being in a position to receive a miracle is realizing that miracles should ultimately point us back to God and our need for Him. We continue returning to Christ and that can change someone else's life! What an amazing gift.

Instead of making miracles the focal point of our faith, our faith should always be placed in God. We can trust in His provision for our lives and know that His timing and plan are always working for the ultimate good.

Avoid making miracles
your idol, but live your life
in a posture that keeps
you open to the miracles
that God may have
in store for you!

I was preaching one time at the high school stadium in Weatherford, Texas, which is a rapidly growing town west of Fort Worth, and when I started talking about how God will use us anywhere—even in parking lots and at Dairy Queens—all of a sudden about ten kids right down in the front row jumped up and started walking out of the stadium.

"Hey, where y'all going?" I asked.

They pointed toward the end of the stadium and said, "The Dairy Queen's right over there. We're going to get all the kids."

I just laughed and kept on preaching.

With maybe ten minutes left in my message, I looked off to the side and saw about twenty or thirty kids walking into the stadium with the young people who had left to go witnessing. They mingled in with the crowd and sat down. When I gave the invitation, most of these kids came forward together and accepted Christ.

WHEN EVENING CAME, MANY WHO WERE DEMON-POSSESSED WERE BROUGHT TO HIM, AND HE DROVE OUT THE SPIRITS WITH A WORD AND HEALED ALL THE SICK. THIS WAS TO FULFILL WHAT WAS SPOKEN THROUGH THE PROPHET ISAIAH: "HE TOOK UP OUR INFIRMITIES AND BORE OUR DISEASES."

Matthew 8:16-17 (NIV)

In my third year of med school, I was required to do a three-mile run. A hundred yards from the finish line, something happened with my legs. It felt like someone punctured a balloon. As soon as I crossed that finish line, I fell to the ground and I was foaming at the mouth. They thought it was heat exhaustion, but after getting water on me, they realized something was seriously wrong.

I was taken to the emergency room where they found I had a 108-degree temperature. At that temperature, you start to cook your brain! My urine turned the color of coffee. It turns out that the muscles in my thighs had ruptured, and I started excreting the myoglobin muscle pigment through my urine, which caused acute kidney failure, which then caused my muscles to literally shrivel up. And over the next couple of weeks I was on high dose IVs in the hospital to save my kidneys! I almost died.

The pain was excruciating. I literally watched as my legs shrunk to be smaller than my arms. They biopsied my thigh—the whole muscle all the way from the top to the bone. When the doctors had results, my wife told them, "Tell me first. Do not say anything in front of my husband."

When the doctor came in, he told me I would never walk again. He said, "Your muscles are dead from the surface of the muscle all the way to the bone." My wife said, "I told you not to tell him that! You're all fired! Now get out of here." She fired my doctors! My wife left the room crying and heard a voice that said, "He shall run and not be weary. He shall walk and not faint." She came back, shook her finger at me and said, "Man has spoken this to you, but God says you shall run and not be weary.

You shall walk and not faint."

I would listen to R. W. Schambach while in the hospital. He inspired faith and belief and expectancy in me. And one day I felt the power of God. I got up. I started walking. It hurt like crazy. The nurses and doctors were amazed. They said, "It's a miracle! Because we have the path report. Those muscles are dead."

No medical explanation—just God. Even though it hurt and even though I was weak, I had to act and I had to expect.

Excerpted from LIFE TODAY *taping with Dr. Don Colbert, January 1, 2018.*

ACT ...

When we act in faith, we open the
door to the possibility of a miracle.
May we always act out of faith rather
than fear. May we always stay open
to the miraculous possibilities that
God has in store for our lives.

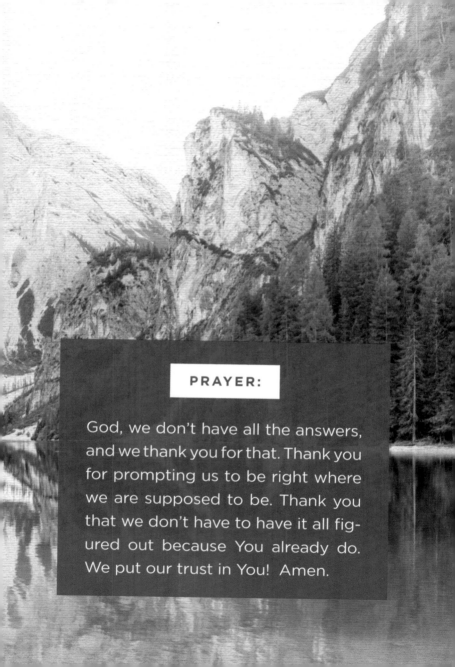

PRAYER:

God, we don't have all the answers, and we thank you for that. Thank you for prompting us to be right where we are supposed to be. Thank you that we don't have to have it all figured out because You already do. We put our trust in You! Amen.

I'm believing right now that as we ask God to be a miracle in our lives, we're going to come to understand more fully than ever that the best way to get our prayers answered is to seek to be an answer to someone else's prayer, be the instrument of God, be His hands, be His love right now and reach out and touch someone. Isaiah 58 is so appropriate for when we allow the power of God to break the bond of oppression, affliction, defeat, set captives free, and we begin to look beyond ourselves and meet the needs of others; He says, "I'm going to answer quickly." And then the miracle; you'll be a well-watered garden. You talk about soaring! You know where it all starts? God, set me free to do Your will, to soar, and to be an answer to someone else's prayer.

He enables us to wait for His perfect timing.

A MAN WAS THERE WHO HAD BEEN ILL FOR THIRTY-EIGHT YEARS. WHEN JESUS SAW HIM LYING THERE, AND KNEW THAT HE HAD ALREADY BEEN A LONG TIME IN THAT CONDITION, HE SAID TO HIM, "DO YOU WISH TO GET WELL?" THE SICK MAN ANSWERED HIM, "SIR, I HAVE NO MAN TO PUT ME INTO THE POOL WHEN THE WATER IS STIRRED UP, BUT WHILE I AM COMING, ANOTHER STEPS DOWN BEFORE ME." JESUS SAID TO HIM, "GET UP, PICK UP YOUR PALLET AND WALK." IMMEDIATELY THE MAN BECAME WELL, AND PICKED UP HIS PALLET AND BEGAN TO WALK.

John 5:5-9 (NASB)

When Annabel was 4-5 years old, she was diagnosed with two incurable intestinal disorders. She was in severe pain; drinking and eating was a challenge. She was in and out of the hospital a lot. The last year of her disorder she was hospitalized nine times, no less than five days each time.

One day she decided to go play outside with her sisters. They were climbing an old cottonwood tree and decided to climb about 30 feet up and sit on a branch. That branch began to give way. Annabel fell head first into the hollow center of the tree.

One of Annabel's sisters dropped a light down to her. She said she dropped it in, but it kept going and going—all 30 feet down to the bottom.

Annabel said, "I wasn't really afraid. I went up to heaven and I remember that it was very bright and I didn't really know where I was until I saw my Mimi who had passed a couple years back. It kind of registered—I must be in heaven. So I sat on Jesus' lap and He told me I was going to be okay. What I thought at the time was no bumps or bruises or a fractured neck because I had fallen head first."

The firefighters spent 3 hours getting Annabel out of the tree—a rescue like they had never done before. Annabel was very calm and peaceful—they said they had never seen anything like it.

When they brought Annabel to the hospital, they ran many, many tests. The doctor said, "Jesus must have been with that little girl in that tree." There wasn't even a bug bite. She was scratched and muddy, but no broken bones, no nothing.

Looking back now, we see that Jesus meant she would be healed. When she went into the tree, she was on ten medications to make her system work poorly at best. And she is on nothing now.

The doctors don't know—they can't explain it. They don't understand—they have no explanation. But they just say that they're sure happy that she fell in that tree.

God works miracles in ways we never could have imagined.

Excerpted from LIFE TODAY *taping with Christy & Annabel Beam, April 20, 2015.*

IMMANUEL . . .

The miracle that is Christ's life is such a
blessing for all of us. From His birth to
His ministry on earth to His miraculous
sacrificial death and resurrection, Christ
is our ultimate miracle. Immanuel—
God with us—He is here with us as
we navigate the waters of life.

Therefore the Lord Himself will give you a sign:
the virgin will conceive and give birth to a son,
and will call him Immanuel (Isaiah 7:14, NIV).

PRAYER:

Thank you, God, for being near to the brokenhearted. Thank you for Your just rule as King over all creation. We are so grateful to know that there is no problem too big for You to handle, no miracle too great for You to work. You are here with us. You know our hearts even better than we do and we thank you! Amen.

Our God is still active.

He is still in the miracle business. He is still not only changing lives, He is changing circumstances and healing people.

Excerpted from LIFE TODAY *taping with Lee Strobel, February 1, 2018.*

"THESE MIRACULOUS SIGNS
WILL ACCOMPANY THOSE WHO BELIEVE:
THEY WILL CAST OUT DEMONS IN MY NAME,
AND THEY WILL SPEAK IN NEW LANGUAGES.
THEY WILL BE ABLE TO HANDLE SNAKES
WITH SAFETY, AND IF THEY DRINK ANYTHING
POISONOUS, IT WON'T HURT THEM.
THEY WILL BE ABLE TO PLACE THEIR HANDS
ON THE SICK, AND THEY WILL BE HEALED."

Mark 16:17-18 (NLT)

"God's miracles are to be
found in nature itself;
the wind and waves,
the wood that becomes a tree
—all of these are explained
biologically, but behind them
is the hand of God."

- Ronald Reagan

INSIGHT SIX:

THE MIRACLE OF LIFE OUTREACH

As I've shared, God has shown me time and time again throughout my life that miracles continue to happen today. Jesus did miraculous things during His time on earth, and I have witnessed equally miraculous things during my lifetime.

One of the most special miracles I have

ever witnessed and had the privilege of being a part of is the miracle of the formation of LIFE Outreach International.

Not only did God use me to travel the world and preach to millions, but then He called me to sit with Betty in front of a camera and call the family of God into the family room. He called me to share the Father's heart from a new platform which would still allow me to reach people around the world.

The miracle of LIFE Outreach is the story of Betty and I connecting with our good friend and missionary partner, Peter Pretorius and his wife, Ann. And this miracle is one of the reasons why I continue to live amazed every single day. From the smallest beginnings, God has orchestrated one of the most amazing things I've ever had the honor of being a part of. What a special thing to see unfold—more amazing and life-changing than I ever could have imagined.

After hearing about Peter's compassion for a pastor in the United States, I knew I wanted to visit this South African missionary.

When Betty and I went to meet Peter, he showed us different areas of need—true, desperate need for clean water and food; the basic sustenance of life.

We traveled into some refugee areas in trucks we had to push-start to get them to run, and when I saw all the kids who were dying while trying to get somewhere safe, it broke my heart and changed my life forever.

God was beginning to work one of the greatest miracles of my life . . .

"I feel like it was in God's beautiful plan when He put it on our heart to reach out in missions. That He had planted Peter and Ann there to partner together so we could express more of our love and God's love to people, to be more effective."

- Betty Robison

WORD OF ENCOURAGEMENT:

Let us be reminded that as members of the body of Christ, we are equipped and enabled through the Holy Spirit to lay hands on people and pray for them. **God can use us as instruments** of His heavenly power to be someone's miracle. Let us always remember to pray for those around us and minister to their needs.

HE SAID TO THEM,
"BECAUSE OF YOUR LITTLE FAITH.
FOR TRULY, I SAY TO YOU, IF YOU HAVE
FAITH LIKE A GRAIN OF MUSTARD SEED,
YOU WILL SAY TO THIS MOUNTAIN,
'MOVE FROM HERE TO THERE,'
AND IT WILL MOVE, AND NOTHING
WILL BE IMPOSSIBLE FOR YOU."

Matthew 17:20 (ESV)

PETER: You know, I was in one area for ten days and more than 300 people died of starvation. For me, that was extremely traumatic. I came back and we managed to put together three truckloads of food, which we took up on a convoy.

And when we got it there and we distributed the food, it was gone in like two hours. One ration to every person and the food was finished. I came to the instant realization that I cannot do this thing on my own. I said to the Lord, "I can't do this on my own. It is not possible. I don't have the money, I don't have the means. I have the willingness. There is a desire in my heart to help. I can't take seeing children die of starvation, but I can't do this on my own."

It was just a little while after that that God sent you [James and Betty] on your mission to South Africa and we met. From then it's been this partnership that has saved the lives of at least 13 million children.

ANNE: It really was miraculous, and it was an answer to our prayers because we realized that you had influence and an audience that we didn't have.

It was a case of complementary gifting working together for the greater purpose for the Kingdom of God.

We as the body of Christ are the means

to be able to reach out and accomplish what Jesus came for. There's no greater privilege than to know that He is utilizing us.

Excerpted from LIFE TODAY *taping with Peter & Ann Pretorius, December 28, 2017.*

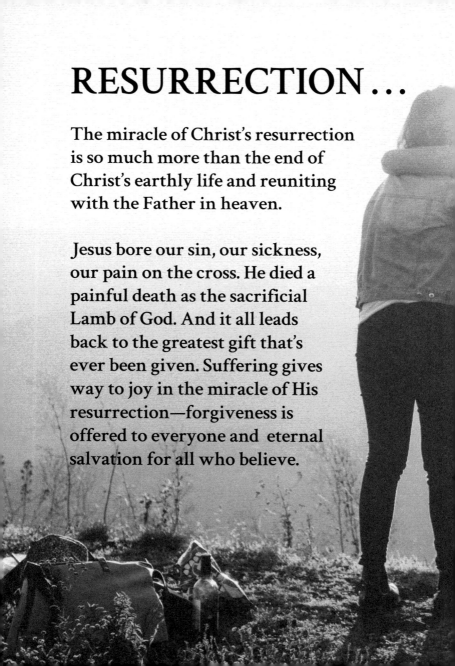

RESURRECTION...

The miracle of Christ's resurrection is so much more than the end of Christ's earthly life and reuniting with the Father in heaven.

Jesus bore our sin, our sickness, our pain on the cross. He died a painful death as the sacrificial Lamb of God. And it all leads back to the greatest gift that's ever been given. Suffering gives way to joy in the miracle of His resurrection—forgiveness is offered to everyone and eternal salvation for all who believe.

PRAYER:

God, open our eyes to the miracles You bring to us in the form of our relationships. Sometimes You place someone in our life who provides a miracle connection, has the resource or provision that is needed, or You bring someone to us with a special ability. We know that it's all for Your Kingdom. Let us partner with the special people You place in our lives and bring the miraculous to earth! Amen.

I told Peter, "Betty and I will move over here and help you." "Please don't," he said. "Please go home and get us the help and support we need so we can stay here to help these people and not be empty-handed." I told our leadership that I was going to ask our LIFE Today viewers if they would help. We began to show people the need and returned many times to all the hard-hit areas of Africa. With oversight from Peter Pretorius, LIFE Outreach

began feeding more than five hundred thousand children a week,

building emergency hospital units and care facilities, and getting emergency medical supplies into clinics in the bush. With Peter's help, we also built the largest orphanage in Rwanda.

I WILL GIVE THANKS TO YOU,
FOR I AM FEARFULLY
AND WONDERFULLY MADE;
WONDERFUL ARE YOUR WORKS,
AND MY SOUL KNOWS IT VERY WELL.

Psalm 139:14 (NASB)

Life Outreach International photographer for more than 30 years, Janice Meyer shared a story from the mission field:

All over the world we have seen things that just break your heart. In one area, we encountered woman after woman who had lost children, and one lady came up to us and said her name was Landy. She had a little house that was made out of cardboard and a few t-shirts and it was so small.

She said, "Please take my child! Please take my child because she's going to die. My other child died, and she is showing the same symptoms." And if that was one story it would break your heart . . . but it was story after story, mother after mother, sister after sister, and that really does break your heart.

But we have an answer. It really is not difficult.

We're the ones that get the blessing. What I saw in a little village—we ended up camping out in this little village in Africa as a well was being drilled. We saw them drill and then they put a little stump on there. And the people were walking by that well to go get water. They were digging a hole to get dirty water. We kept telling them, "You don't have to go to the dry river bed to get water anymore. It is going to come out right there." They couldn't believe us because that was like telling them that there were Martians; that's how foreign it was to them. "No, I've gone to the river since I was a baby. So you can't tell me there's going to be water coming out of that thing. I don't even know what it is."

The next day we put the pump on it. And these ladies —one lady had the biggest smile you've ever seen. It was a miracle for them!

This one lady said, "God is big!" I said, "Yes, He is! Yes, He is! He wants to be big for everybody." But they couldn't even believe it. She said, "I still have to go down to the river, right?" And we said, "No! Never again! Now you have clean water."

You know what it will do for that village? Everything! It changes it from death to life. Now they'll watch their children—they won't even believe how healthy. They have never seen their children that healthy! And that can happen everywhere!

Excerpted from LIFE TODAY *taping July 22, 2011.*

SENSITIVE . . .

When we are sensitive to the prompting of the Holy Spirit, it's amazing what the Lord can do. God gives us wonderful opportunities!

. . . sometimes we want our miracle, we need our miracle, but I found that sometimes the quickest way to the miracle that you need is to realize that you're someone else's miracle. If you'll focus on just being that miracle for another person, then it's amazing how it comes back around and God blesses us.

– Mark Batterson

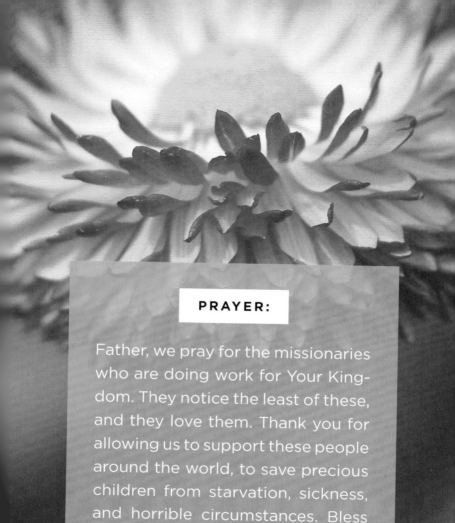

PRAYER:

Father, we pray for the missionaries who are doing work for Your Kingdom. They notice the least of these, and they love them. Thank you for allowing us to support these people around the world, to save precious children from starvation, sickness, and horrible circumstances. Bless these missionaries, the work they do, and the lives they touch. Amen.

To our amazement, when we shared on our television show the opportunities on the mission field, not only did our viewers want to help, but they also encouraged us to take on other ventures. For instance, **viewers suggested that we drill water wells,** because it was so obvious everywhere we went that there was no clean water.

"AND WHOEVER GIVES
ONE OF THESE LITTLE ONES
ONLY A CUP OF COLD WATER
IN THE NAME OF A DISCIPLE,
ASSUREDLY, I SAY TO YOU,
HE SHALL BY NO MEANS
LOSE HIS REWARD."

Matthew 10:42 (NKJV)

IT'S ONE PERSON AT A TIME

WE ARE SO THANKFUL
FOR THE VIEWERS OF LIFE TODAY
BECAUSE THEY SEE THE NEEDS
AND THEY MEET THEM.
THE MIRACLE IS REALLY THE VIEWERS.
WHEN ONE PERSON SAYS,
"I'LL HELP THREE KIDS," OR
"I'LL HELP YOU WITH TEN KIDS,"
THAT'S THE MIRACLE—

THAT'S THE
MIRACLE OF LOVE.

I believe we all have been invited to journey with Christ. God chose me. He also chose you. Will He put you on the same path He's put me on? Likely not. But I believe everyone has the potential to witness the things I have witnessed. I don't say this to compare your successes, failures, weaknesses, and strengths with mine. I simply mean that the Lord can and will do amazing things through your life, just has He has done through mine.

— *James Robison*